My First BIG Book of DINOSAUR FACTS

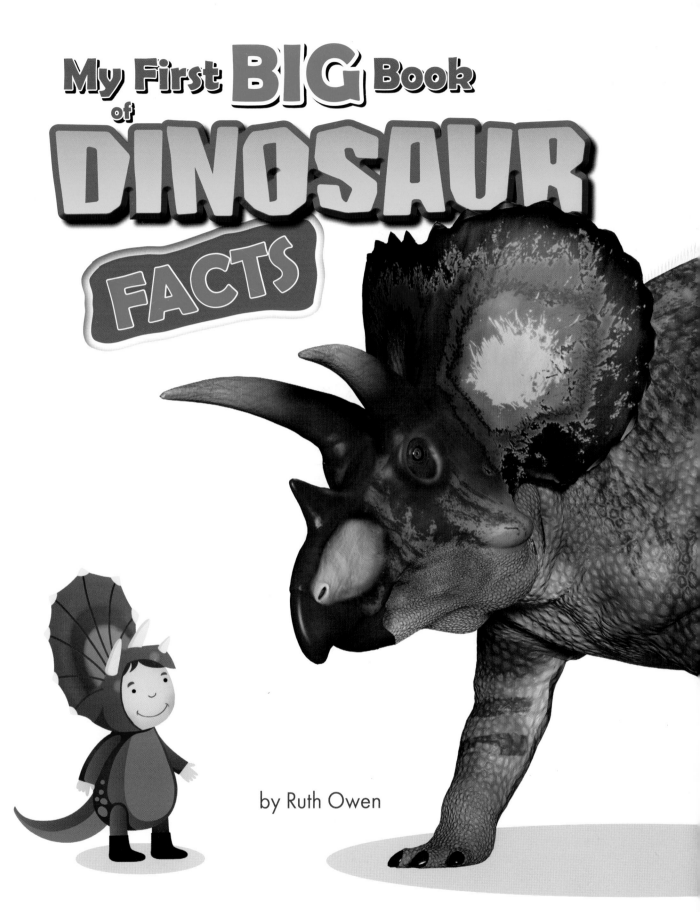

by Ruth Owen

Ruby Tuesday Books

Published in 2022 by Ruby Tuesday Books Ltd.

Designer: Emma Randall
Editor: Mark J. Sachner
Production: John Lingham

Photo credits:
Alamy: 44–45 (Chris Stock Photography), 46 top (DPA Picture Alliance), 77 (Steve Vidler); David A. Burnham: 33 bottom; Tom Connell: 12–13, 14–15; Gregory M. Erickson: 60; Aaron Fredlund: 69 bottom; istockphoto: 23; James Kuether: Cover, 1, 4, 5, 6–7, 17, 27, 29 bottom, 31, 32, 33 top, 35 bottom, 36–37 bottom, 39, 41, 50–51, 52 top, 53, 54–55, 57, 68, 72–73, 74–75, 76, 79 bottom, 80 bottom, 81, 82–83, 84, 86–87, 88 top, 92–93; Kenneth Lacovara: 18, 19 bottom; Shutterstock: Cover (W. Scott McGill), 3, 6–7, 10 bottom (W. Scott McGill), 11 bottom (Andrej Antic), 16, 19 top, 20, 24, 25 bottom (Lucas Krbec), 28 (Sergey Uryadnikov), 30, 34, 36–37 top, 38, 40, 42, 46 bottom, 54 top right, 64, 66–67, 71 (Jaroslav Moravcik), 72 top, 78, 85 middle (Akkharat Jarusilawong), 86 top, 88 bottom, 91; Shutterstock/Daniel Eskridge: 65, 85 bottom, 90; Shutterstock/Herschel Hoffmeyer: 8–9, 43, 47, 59, 61, 63, 89; Shutterstock/Michael Rosskothen: 2, 80 top; Superstock: 49; Superstock/Francois Gohier: 21 top, 22, 25 top, 58; Superstock/Steve Vidler: 48.

Library of Congress Control Number: 2021919969
Print (hardback) ISBN 978-1-78856-246-1
Print (paperback) ISBN 978-1-78856-247-8
eBook PDF ISBN 978-1-78856-248-5
ePub ISBN 978-1-78856-249-2

Published in Minneapolis, MN, United States

www.rubytuesdaybooks.com

What's Inside?

What Is a Dinosaur?

A dinosaur is an animal that lived millions of years ago.

Dinosaurs came in many different shapes and sizes.

Velociraptor

Some dinosaurs walked on two legs, and some walked on four.

Dinosaurs belonged to an animal group called **reptiles**.

Giraffatitan

There are still reptiles alive today. Crocodiles, alligators, lizards, snakes, and turtles are all reptiles.

When Did Dinosaurs Live on Earth?

Dinosaurs lived on Earth MILLIONS AND MILLIONS AND MILLIONS AND MILLIONS AND MILLIONS AND MILLIONS AND MILLIONS AND MILLIONS AND MILLIONS AND MILLIONS AND MILLIONS AND MILLIONS OF YEARS AGO!

We call the time when the dinosaurs lived prehistoric times.

Get ready for some BIG dino numbers!

Scientists think dinosaurs first lived on Earth about **240 million** years ago.

They were the main animals on Earth for around **170 million** years.

Then, about **66 million** years ago, most dinosaurs died out.

This is called becoming **extinct**.

Let's say it! "ex-TINK-t"

Did People Live at the Time of the Dinosaurs?

No! Dinosaurs lived on Earth millions of years before there were people.

Tyrannosaurus rex

Sometimes TV shows and movies show dinosaurs and **cave people** living together.

But this didn't happen in real life.

A caveman

Phew! I'm glad we don't live with dinosaurs. Some of them look really scary!

9

How Do We Know There Were Dinosaurs?

Dinosaurs became extinct millions of years ago.

But they left behind some clues that they were here.

Sometimes people find dinosaur bones called **fossils** inside rocks.

Fossil dinosaur bones

Dinosaur horns, teeth, and claws also turned into fossils.

A fossil *Velociraptor* claw

Fresh bones are white and not very heavy.

A wolf skull and teeth

Fresh bones

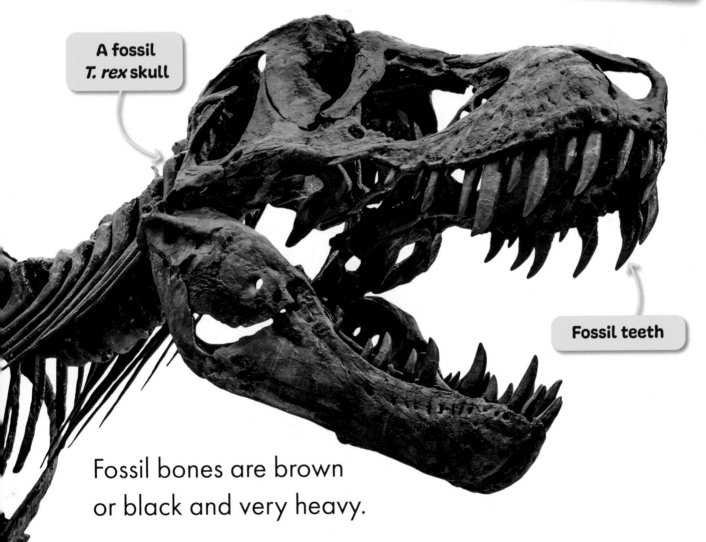

A fossil *T. rex* skull

Fossil teeth

Fossil bones are brown or black and very heavy.

That's because the bones have turned to rock!

How Did Dinosaurs Become Fossils?

Not every dinosaur became a fossil. But luckily for us, some did. How did this happen?

An old or sick dinosaur lay down by a river and died.

Other animals ate the soft meaty parts of its body.

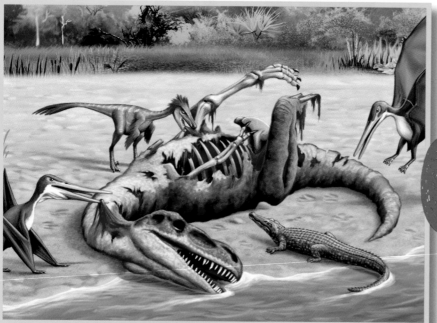

Sometimes other animals carried off parts of the dinosaur to eat!

Soon, only bones were left.

The bones were washed into the river by heavy rain.

They sank to the riverbed and were buried in mud.

What Happened Next to the Dinosaur's Bones?

**Thousands of years passed by.
More layers of mud covered the bones.**

The river dried up, and the mud changed to rock.
This took millions of years!

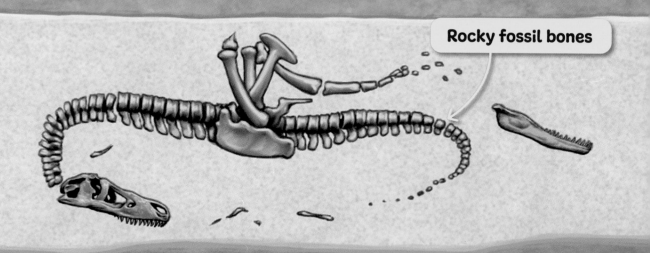

Rocky fossil bones

The dinosaur's bones also
changed and became rock.

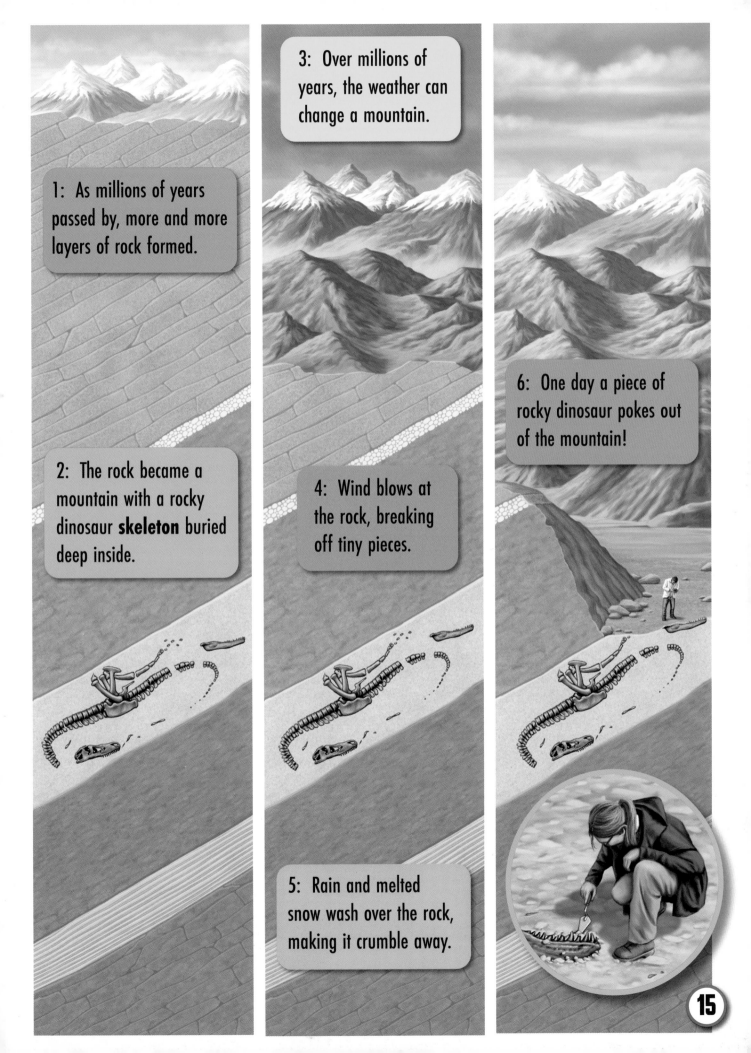

1: As millions of years passed by, more and more layers of rock formed.

2: The rock became a mountain with a rocky dinosaur **skeleton** buried deep inside.

3: Over millions of years, the weather can change a mountain.

4: Wind blows at the rock, breaking off tiny pieces.

5: Rain and melted snow wash over the rock, making it crumble away.

6: One day a piece of rocky dinosaur pokes out of the mountain!

Did Dino Poops Become Fossils?

Yes! People don't only dig up **fossilized** dinosaur bones. They also find prehistoric dino poop.

Dinosaur coprolites

A poop that has become a rocky fossil is called a **coprolite**.

Scientists think this coprolite belonged to a *Tyrannosaurus rex*.

People have found *T. rex* coprolites
that are 20 inches (50 cm) long!

That's a lot of dino doo-doo!

Prehistoric poop
is very helpful to scientists.
Can you guess why?

You will find out
later in the book.

What Are Scientists Who Study Fossils Called?

Scientists who dig up and study fossils are called **paleontologists**.

Kenneth Lacovara is a paleontologist. He discovered a giant dinosaur called *Dreadnoughtus*.

Kenneth Lacovara

A *Dreadnoughtus* leg bone

Let's say it! "Pay-lee-on-TOL-uh-gist"

Paleontologists look for fossils on the slopes of mountains and cliffs.

Rocky cliffs

If they find one fossil, they try to find the rest of the dinosaur.

Fossil tailbones of *Oreadnoughtus*

The place where fossils are dug up is called a dig site.

What Happens at a Dino Dig?

Paleontologists dig up the rock where the fossils are buried.

Sometimes they use a digger to remove big chunks of rock.

They dig with jackhammers, pickaxes, and spades.

Pickax

Spade

Jackhammer

Then they carefully remove the rock close to the fossils.

Brush

Trowel

Chisel

They do this with small trowels, chisels, and brushes.

Paleontologist

Fossil

Paleontologists draw a map of a dig site. This shows where each fossil was found.

A dig map

How Are Fossils Protected?

Sometimes paleontologists dig up large fossils inside a lump of rock.

A *Tyrannosaurus rex* fossil in rock

Plaster jacket

They cover the fossil and rock in a **plaster** jacket. As the jacket dries, it gets hard and protects the fossil.

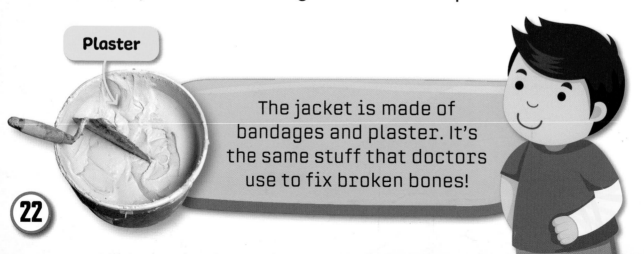

Plaster

The jacket is made of bandages and plaster. It's the same stuff that doctors use to fix broken bones!

Paleontologists take the fossils they find to a museum.

The plaster jacket has been cut open.

This scientist is using a small tool to blast the rock away from the fossil.

What Happens to Fossils?

A paleontologist looks carefully at the size and shape of a fossil.

They try to figure out what kind of dinosaur the fossil belongs to.

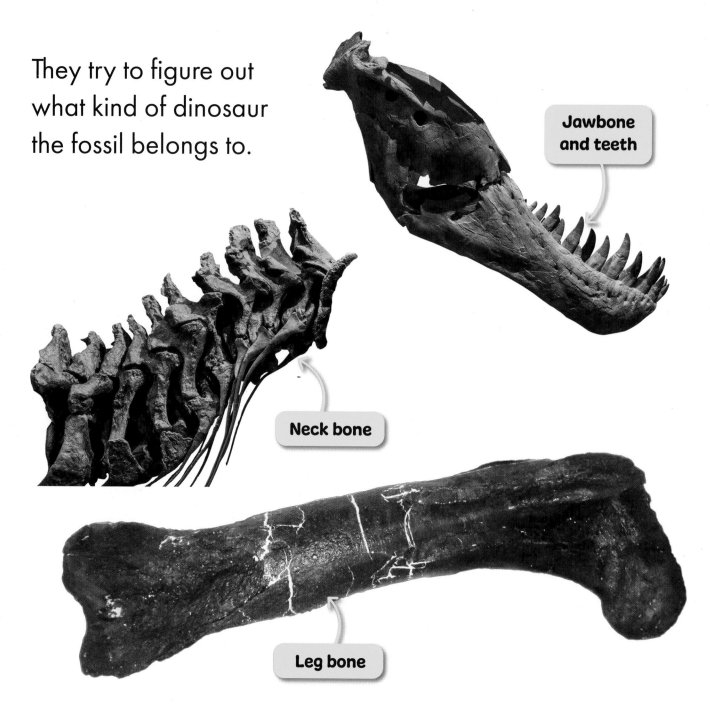

Jawbone and teeth

Neck bone

Leg bone

Sometimes fossils can tell us about a dinosaur's life.

Big, sharp teeth show that a dinosaur ate meat.

A *T. rex* tooth

If scientists find lots of fossils from a dinosaur, they fit them together.

A *Triceratops* skeleton

It's like doing a giant jigsaw puzzle!

Then people can see the dinosaur skeleton in a museum.

Who Invented the Word "Dinosaur"?

The word "dinosaur" was invented by a scientist named Sir Richard Owen.

He lived more than 170 years ago.

Richard Owen carefully looked at lots of different fossils.

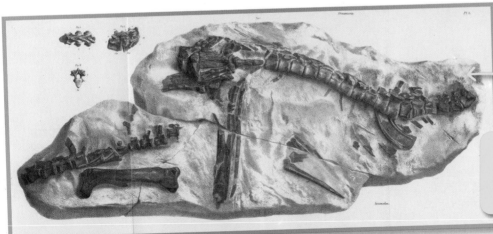

Richard Owen's drawing of *Iguanodon* fossils

He realized that the prehistoric creatures all belonged to one animal group.

In 1842, Richard Owen gave the group a name:

DINOSAURS!

An *Alamosaurus*

The word means "fearfully great, or big, lizards."

Who Made the First Dinosaur Model?

Richard Owen and other scientists studied their dinosaur fossils.

They looked at living reptiles such as crocodiles and lizards.

A Komodo dragon lizard

Then they guessed how the prehistoric animals looked.

In 1854, a **sculptor** made giant models of some dinosaurs. Richard Owen helped.

They thought *Iguanodon* looked like this. It was a good first guess!

The sculptor's name was Benjamin Waterhouse Hawkins.

Since then, scientists have found more *Iguanodon* fossils.

Iguanodon

Today, scientists think it looked like this.

How Do Dinosaurs Get Their Names?

The scientist who finds a new kind of dinosaur gets to give it a name!

Scientists use a very old language called Latin to name dinosaurs.

Triceratops fossil

The name *Triceratops* means "three-horned face" in Latin.

The name *Pachycephalosaurus* means "thick-headed lizard" in Latin.

These dinosaurs used their heads as battering rams.

Pachycephalosaurus

A *Pachycephalosaurus* had a skull that was 10 inches (25 cm) thick!

Let's say it!
"pak-ee-SEFF-al-oh-SAW-russ"

Did Dinosaurs Eat Each Other?

Yes, they did! Some dinosaurs were carnivores, or meat-eaters.

They hunted plant-eating dinosaurs and each other.

Deinonychus

Some meat-eaters, such as Deinonychus, ate dinosaurs that were already dead.

Sometimes big Deinonychus ate little ones!

Scientists think *Tyrannosaurus rex* hunted plant-eaters and fed on dead bodies.

T. rex

Edmontosaurus

Paleontologists found a *T. rex* tooth in the fossil tailbone of a plant-eater called *Edmontosaurus*.

Fossil tail bone

T. rex tooth

What Was on the Menu for Plant-Eaters?

Plant-eating dinosaurs ate tough prehistoric plants.

Triceratops ate flowers, ferns and low-growing **cycads**, and palm trees.

Cycad

Prehistoric plants were tough to chew.

Palm tree

Triceratops teeth wore out quickly.

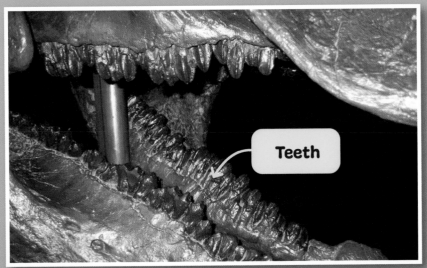

Teeth

Triceratops had a stack of teeth in its mouth.

When a tooth fell out, a new one took its place.

Triceratops had up to 800 teeth in its mouth at once!

What Did Giant Dinosaurs Eat?

The biggest dinosaurs were the titanosaurs. They ate plants—lots of plants!

Coprolite

Scientists found a titanosaur coprolite.

Inside the fossil poop, there were bits of grass, cycads, palm trees, and **conifer** trees.

This is a titanosaur called *Futalognkosaurus.*

A monkey puzzle conifer tree

The poop clues show that titanosaurs possibly ate plants on the ground and tall trees.

Animals that only eat plants are called **herbivores**.

Where Did Dinosaurs Live?

Dinosaurs lived all over the world. They even lived in Antarctica!

Today, there are hardly any animals in freezing, icy Antarctica.

The South Pole is in Antarctica.

North America

Atlantic Ocean

South America

Pacific Ocean

Antarctica (an-TARK-tic-ah)

Penguins in Antarctica

But millions of years ago, Antarctica was much warmer.

There were forests and meadows, and lots of dinosaurs lived there.

Antarctopelta was a plant-eater.

Antarctopelta

Cryolophosaurus

Cryolophosaurus was a meat-eater.

What Color Were Dinosaurs?

That's a BIG question that scientists can't answer. Yet!

Elephant

Scientists thought that maybe dinosaurs were gray or brown, like some big modern animals.

Rhinoceros

A lizard called a chameleon

But now they think dinosaurs were more colorful, like lizards and birds.

A male *Triceratops'* big frill was for showing off to other males.

Triceratops

It makes sense that it would have lots of colors and patterns.

Was T. rex Striped and Feathery?

No one can say for sure. Yet!

Tiger

Some scientists think *Tyrannosaurus rex* hunted like a tiger.

It hid in forests, watching its **prey**. Then it attacked!

Maybe *T. rex* had striped **camouflage** to help it hide among plants.

Fossils show that *T. rex* had **scales** on its body.

Feathers

Scales

But some of *T. rex*'s dinosaur relatives had feathers.

Maybe *T. rex* also had some feathers on its body.

Which Dinosaur Was the Biggest?

In 2014, paleontologists dug up about 130 big fossils.

The fossils came from the biggest dinosaur that has ever been found!

The paleontologists named it *Patagotitan*.

Let's say it! "pat-a-go-TIE-tun"

This is a life-size model of *Patagotitan*.

The giant dino is named after Patagonia, the place where it was found.

Patagotitan grew up to 121 feet (37 m) long

Who Was the Biggest Meat-Eater?

Spinosaurus was a huge meat-eater that was longer than a bus!

The spines on its back were as tall as a grown-up.

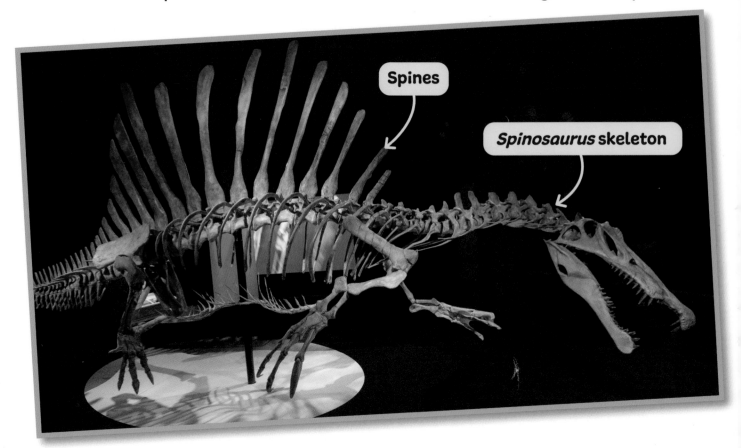

Spines

Spinosaurus skeleton

This fossil *Spinosaurus* tooth is real life-size.

The spines were covered with skin.

Spines

Spinosaurus lived in water and on land, like a crocodile.

Spinosaurus

This dinosaur's name means "spine lizard."

Which Dino Was the Smallest?

One of the smallest dinosaurs was called *Microraptor*.

It was smaller than a chicken.

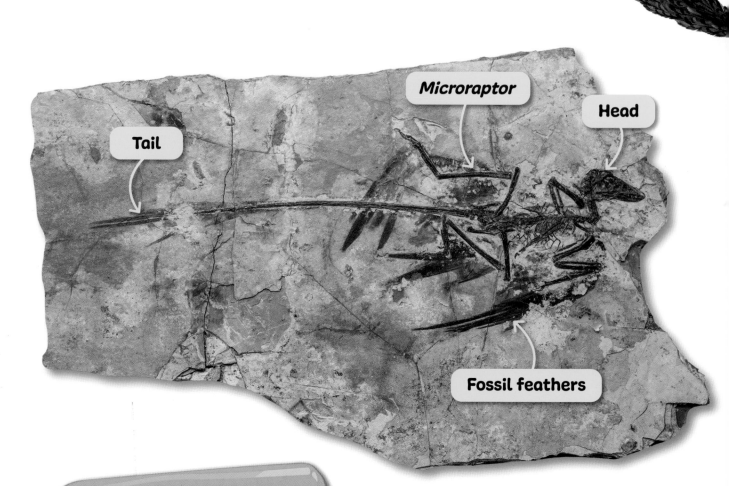

Tail

Microraptor

Head

Fossil feathers

Scientists found fossil *Microraptors* with food in their stomachs.

The fossilized food included fish scales, prehistoric birds, and a whole lizard.

Microraptors had wings, feathers, and a long tail.

Microraptor

Many scientists think they could fly.

The name *Microraptor* means "small one who grabs by force."

Why Did Dinosaurs Have Horns?

A male _Triceratops_ used his long horns for fighting.

Triceratops lived in **herds** that were led by a big male.

If another male wanted to be leader, there was a fight!

The horns on the top of a _Triceratops'_ head were 3 feet (1 m) long!

The two dinosaurs rammed their horns together.

The winner of the fight became herd leader.

Male *Triceratops*

Which Dinosaur Had the Most Horns?

Triceratops had three horns, but some of its relatives had lots more.

A dinosaur called *Styracosaurus* had a long nose horn.

Styracosaurus

It also had six horns around its frill.

A fossil *Kosmoceratops* skull

Kosmoceratops had 15 horns!

Kosmoceratops had a nose horn and two cheek horns.

It also had two long horns on its head and ten short horns on its frill.

Which Dino Had a Crash-Helmet Head?

A plant-eating dinosaur called *Stegoceras* had a skull shaped like a bike helmet!

A fossil *Stegoceras* skull

Bike helmet

Its skull was thick and dome shaped.

A male *Stegoceras* used its head to ram other males.

Scientists think *Stegoceras* had fights over females.

This dino was the same size as a Labrador dog.

Stegoceras

Why Did Stegosaurus Have Spikes?

Stegosaurus was a plant-eater.
It was 30 feet (9 m) long.

It had bony plates
on its back.

Bony plates

Fossil *Stegosaurus*

Spikes

It had spikes on its tail that were
35 inches (90 cm) long!

Scientists don't
know what the plates
were for.

Stegosaurus used its spiky tail to fight off hungry meat-eaters, such as Allosaurus.

Scientists found an Allosaurus fossil with a hole in it. The hole matched the spike on a Stegosaurus tail!

Stegosaurus

Allosaurus

Which Dinosaur Had the Biggest Teeth?

The winner is *Tyrannosaurus rex*. Some of its teeth were 8 inches (20 cm) long!

At the sides of *T. rex*'s huge jaws there were teeth with jagged edges like a saw.

These teeth were for slicing meat off bones.

T. rex tooth

Jagged edge

This *T. rex* tooth is real life-size!

At the front of *T. rex*'s jaws there were thick, stubby teeth. These were for grabbing prey.

BIGGEST TEETH

Which Dino's Bite Was the Most Powerful?

The winner is the champion chomper—*Tyrannosaurus rex*!

Scientists wanted to know how hard *T. rex* could bite.

An alligator

They measured the bites of alligators.

Then they compared the alligators' jaws to a *T. rex*'s jaws.

The scientists figured out that a *T. rex*'s bite could crush a car!

BIGGEST BITE

Some fossil *T. rex* skulls have holes in them. The holes could be bites from another *T. rex*!

Which Dinosaur Had the Longest Claws?

The prize for the longest claws goes to a dino called *Therizinosaurus*.

It had three long claws on each hand.

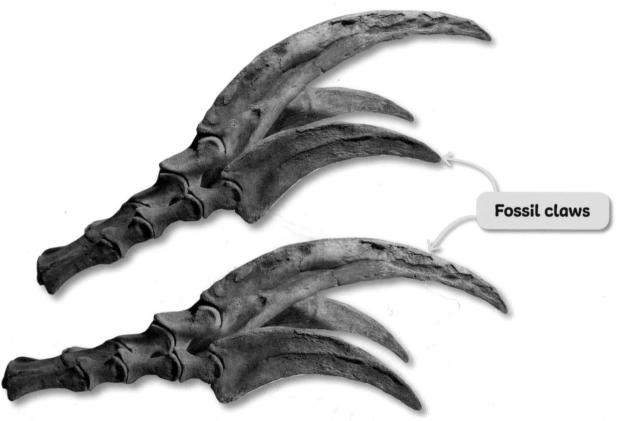

Fossil claws

Therizinosaurus didn't use its claws for hunting because it was a plant-eater.

Let's say it!
"ther-ih-ZEE-no-SAW-rus"

BIGGEST CLAWS

Therizinosaurus

This dinosaur's claws could grow to 3 feet (1 m) long!

What Sounds Did Dinosaurs Make?

This is a very tricky question to answer. But sometimes, fossils can give scientists clues.

A dinosaur called *Parasaurolophus* had a long **crest** on its head.

Crest

Parasaurolophus skull

Scientists think the dinosaur used the crest to make a noise like an organ.

An organ in a church

The dinosaur's crest had hollow tubes inside.

When it breathed air into the tubes, the crest made a loud booming sound.

Parasaurolophus

BOOOOM BOOOOM

Did T. rex Roar?

Lions and tigers have parts in their throats that help them roar. But *T. rex* did not have this.

A scientist named Julia Clark had an idea.

She thinks *T. rex* may have made a noise like an ostrich mixed with a crocodile.

Ostriches make a booming noise.

Crocodiles make a rumbling, growling noise.

Julia Clark put the sounds together.

It made a deep, scary **whumpf, whumpf** noise!

Is this how *T. rex* sounded? No one can say for sure.

Did Dinosaurs Leave Footprints Behind?

Yes! Paleontologists have found rocky dino prints. But how did this happen?

Millions of years ago, a dinosaur stepped in mud and left a giant footprint.

Then the mud turned to rock.

This footprint belonged to a huge plant-eating dinosaur. It is 42 inches (107 cm) long.

Footprint

Paleontologists have carefully dug away the rock around the footprint.

This is a big meat-eating dinosaur's footprint.

Where Did Baby Dinosaurs Come From?

Baby dinosaurs hatched from eggs.

It might seem like a giant dinosaur would lay an egg that's taller than you.

Dreadnoughtus

But the eggs of the biggest dinosaurs were only the size of soccer balls. Why?

Fossil titanosaur egg

The bigger an egg grows,
the thicker its shell gets.

Dinosaur eggs
stayed quite small.

A model of a
Maiasaura nest

This helped the babies inside
break through the shells.

Did Dinosaurs Build Nests?

Yes! Paleontologists have found fossil nests.

These fossil eggs belong to a dino called *Citipati*.

A mother *Maiasaura* dug her nest in soil or sand.

She laid up to 30 eggs in the nest.

The *Maiasaura* covered her eggs with plants to keep them warm.

When the baby dinosaurs hatched, she brought them plants to eat.

The name *Maiasaura* means "good mother lizard."

Mother *Maiasaura*

New babies

One-year-old baby

Nest

Did Giant Dinosaurs Build Nests?

Yes! In Argentina, scientists found about 400 fossil *Saltasaurus* nests.

Saltasaurus digging nest

Laying eggs

Each mother *Saltasaurus* dug a nest in the sandy ground.

She laid up to 40 round eggs inside and left the eggs to hatch.

The nest looked like this.

How Did Dinosaur Eggs Become Fossils?

Each mother *Saltasaurus* laid her eggs near a river.

But after the eggs were laid, the river **flooded**.

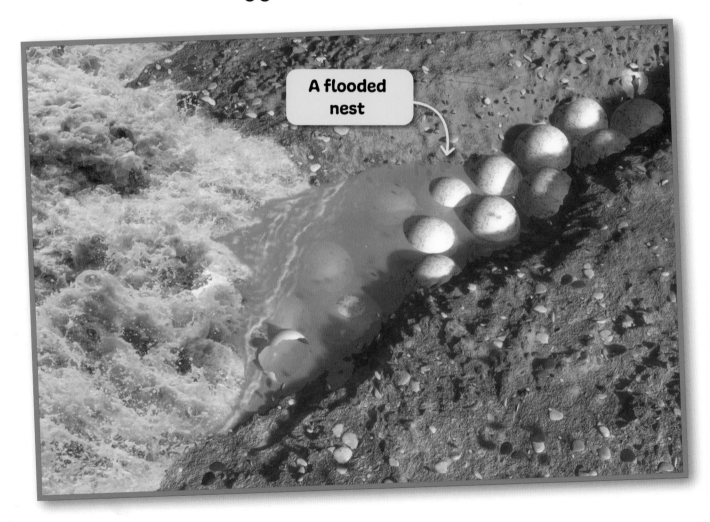

A flooded nest

The eggs were buried in mud.

After a long time, the mud turned to rock and the eggs became fossils.

Scientists dug the fossil eggs from the rock.

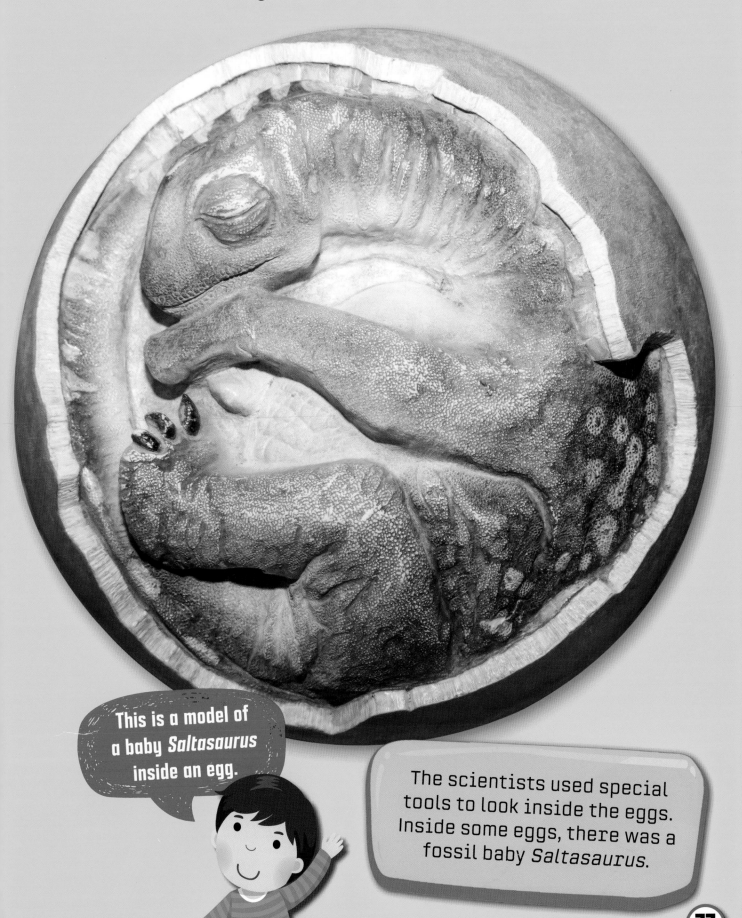

This is a model of a baby *Saltasaurus* inside an egg.

The scientists used special tools to look inside the eggs. Inside some eggs, there was a fossil baby *Saltasaurus*.

What Did Baby Dinosaurs Look Like?

A baby titanosaur, such as *Argentinosaurus*, was small when it hatched.

Scientists think it was about the size of a cat.

Baby *Argentinosaurus*

Once an Argentinosaurus grew up, it was as heavy as 18 elephants!

A baby *Triceratops* had tiny, stumpy horns and a little frill.

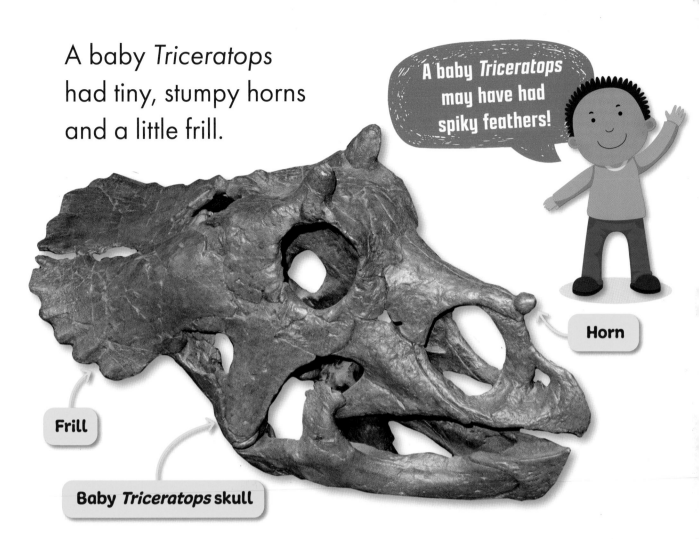

A baby *Triceratops* may have had spiky feathers!

Horn

Frill

Baby *Triceratops* skull

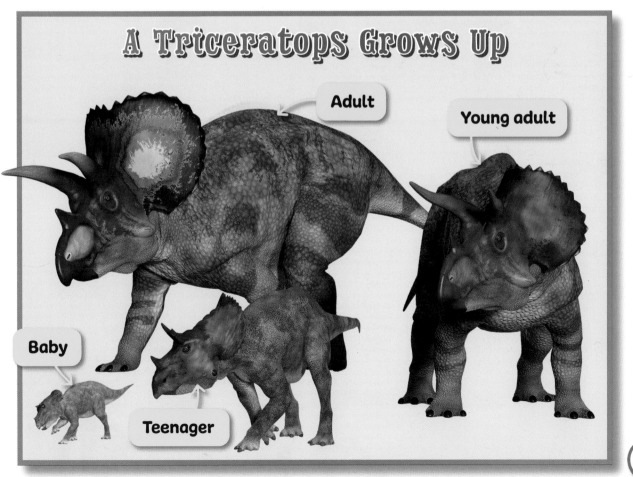

A Triceratops Grows Up

Adult

Young adult

Baby

Teenager

Were There Flying Prehistoric Animals?

At the time of the dinosaurs there were HUGE reptiles that could fly.

A flying reptile called *Quetzalcoatlus* had a **wingspan** of 36 feet (11 m)!

Let's say it! "KWET-sa-COTE-lass"

A flying reptile called *Hatzegopteryx* had a head and beak that was 10 feet (3 m) long.

When it stood on the ground, *Hatzegopteryx* was taller than a double-decker bus!

Let's say it!
"hat-zuh-GOP-ter-ix"

What Did Big Flying Reptiles Eat?

Scientists think that most flying reptiles ate meat and fish.

Hatzegopteryx was one of the biggest flying animals that ever lived.

It hunted for dinosaurs to eat.

Hatzegopteryx

Its wingspan was almost 40 feet (12 m).

Hatzegopteryx had a huge mouth and could swallow a small dinosaur in one gulp!

It used its giant beak to bite and stab its prey.

Did Dinosaurs Live in the Sea?

No! Dinosaurs only lived on land.
But there were giant meat-eating reptiles
in the sea at the time of the dinosaurs.

Liopleurodon crunched up other reptiles in its long jaws.

Liopleurodon

Mosasaurus

Mosasaurus was 56 feet (17 m)
long—that's longer than a bus!

Mary Anning

A fossil hunter named Mary Anning dug up an ocean reptile called *Ichthyosaurus* in 1811.

She found its fossils in the cliffs at Lyme Regis in England.

An *Ichthyosaurus* fossil

Ichthyosaurus means "fish lizard."

What Happened to the Dinosaurs?

About 66 million years ago, a giant space rock called an **asteroid** crashed into Earth!

When the asteroid hit Earth, it landed on the seashore.

Asteroid

The asteroid was about 6 miles (10 km) wide.

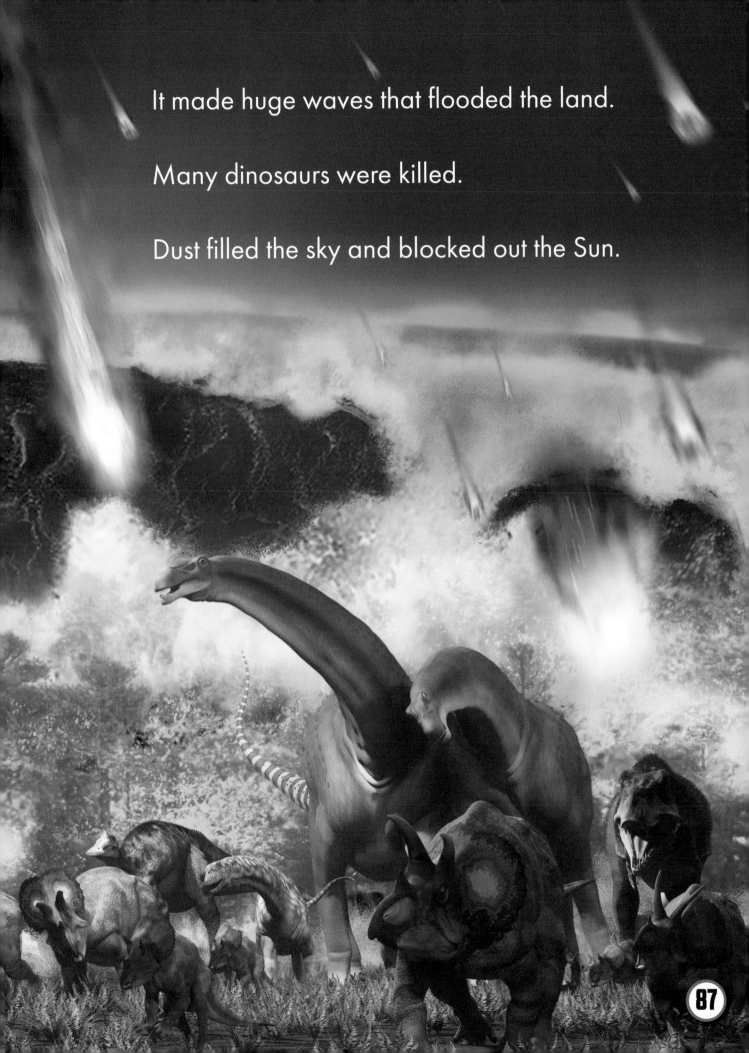

It made huge waves that flooded the land.

Many dinosaurs were killed.

Dust filled the sky and blocked out the Sun.

What Happened After the Asteroid Crash?

After the asteroid crash, the Earth became cold and dark.

Plants stopped growing because there was no sunlight.

Plant-eating dinosaurs died because there were no plants to eat.

Crocodiles lived at the same time as the dinosaurs, but they did not become extinct.

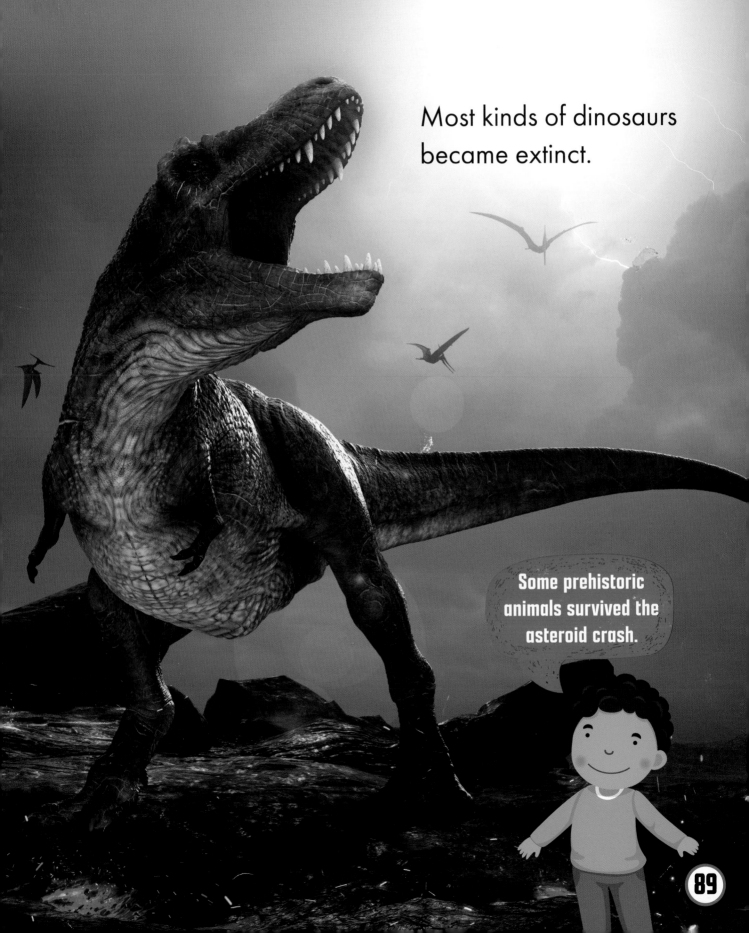

Meat-eating dinosaurs died because there were no plant-eaters to feed on.

Most kinds of dinosaurs became extinct.

Some prehistoric animals survived the asteroid crash.

Are Birds Dinosaurs?

Before the asteroid crash, some dinosaurs were evolving into prehistoric birds.

The word "evolving" means changing bit by bit over a long time.

Archaeopteryx was a prehistoric bird.

Archaeopteryx

Archaeopteryx had teeth and claws like a dinosaur. But it had feathers and could fly like a bird.

Great gray owl

Some prehistoric birds survived the crash and kept on evolving.

They became all the birds we see today.

Turkey

Rhinoceros hornbill

Bullfinch

That's why people say that birds are dinosaurs!

Do We Know Everything About Dinosaurs?

No, we don't. Paleontologists are finding out new things all the time.

When a new fossil is dug up, it can tell us more about a dinosaur's shape.

Sometimes scientists find a fossil from a completely new dinosaur.

Would you like to be a paleontologist?

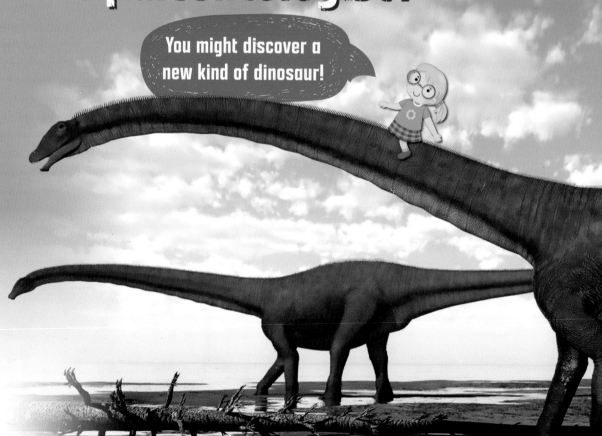

You might discover a new kind of dinosaur!

T. rex

Triceratops

So far, scientists have discovered about 700 different kinds of dinosaurs.

Diplodocus

My Dinosaur Words

asteroid
A giant rock that's flying through space.

camouflage
Colors or patterns on an animal's body that help it blend into its background.

carnivore
An animal that only eats meat.

cave people
People who lived thousands of years ago. They made their homes in rocky caves.

conifer
A tree that grows cones and does not drop its leaves in winter.

coprolite
The poop of an animal from long ago that has become a fossil.

crest
An area made of bone, fur, feathers, or skin on the head of an animal.

cycad
A plant with cones and palm tree-like leaves that grows in a hot place.

extinct
No longer alive and gone forever.

flooded
Covered by lots of water from heavy rains or overflowing rivers.

fossil
The rocky remains of an animal or plant that lived millions of years ago.

fossilized
Turned into a fossil.

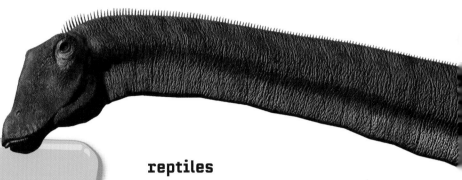

herbivore
An animal that only eats plants.

herd
A group of animals that live together.

paleontologist
A scientist who studies animals and plants from long ago.

plaster
A liquid mix of rock, sand, and water that turns hard when it dries.

prehistoric
A long, long time ago before people began recording history.

prey
An animal this is hunted by other animals for food.

reptiles
An animal group that includes animals such as lizards, snakes, and crocodiles. It also includes the dinosaurs and some other prehistoric animals.

scales
Small, tough, overlapping sections of skin.

sculptor
A person who makes models from stone, wood, and other materials.

skeleton
A framework of bones inside the body of an animal or person.

wingspan
The distance between the tips of two wings.

Big Dino Quiz

1: What are scientists who study fossils called?
- a) Dino-ologists
- b) Paleontologists
- c) Fossilologists

2: What is the biggest dinosaur that's been found?
- a) *Tyrannosaurus rex*
- b) *Maiasaura*
- c) *Patagotitan*

3: What is a fossilized poop called?
- a) A prehistoric plop
- b) A flintstone
- c) A coprolite

4: Which dinosaur had the biggest teeth?
- a) *Spinosaurus*
- b) *Diplodocus*
- c) *Tyrannosaurus rex*

5: What does *Triceratops* mean?
- a) Three-horned face
- b) Top plant eater
- c) Fights with horns

6: What colors were dinosaurs?
- a) Gray and brown
- b) Scientists don't know for sure
- c) Lots of different colors

7: How big was a baby *Argentinosaurus*?
- a) As big as a cat
- b) As big as a cow
- c) As big as an elephant

8: What was *Hatzegopteryx*?
- a) A tiny plant-eating dinosaur
- b) A giant flying reptile
- c) A prehistoric crocodile

9: What killed the dinosaurs?
- a) A big storm
- b) An asteroid crash
- c) Cave people hunting them

10: What did some dinosaurs become?
- a) They became modern-day lizards
- b) They became crocodiles
- c) They became modern-day birds

Answers:
1) b 2) c 3) c 4) c 5) a
6) b 7) a 8) b 9) b 10) c

96